PITFALLS FROM PUT-OFF'S

PITFALLS FROM PUT-OFF'S

Memoirs of a Procrastinator

BRENDA BALLANTINE M.A.

Copyright © 2011 by Brenda D. Ballantine M.A.

Pitfalls From Put-Off's
Memoirs of a procrastinator
by Brenda D. Ballantine M.A.

Printed in the United States of America

ISBN 9781619043237

All rights reserved solely by the author. The author guarantees all contents are original and do not infringe upon the legal rights of any other person or work. No part of this book may be reproduced in any form without the permission of the author. The views expressed in this book are not necessarily those of the publisher.

Disclaimer

This book contains the opinions and ideas of the author. It is intended to provide helpful and informative material on the subject addressed within. It is sold with the knowledge that the author is not engaged in rendering psychological, medical or health, or any other kind of personal or professional services in this book. If the reader requires personal therapeutic or health related assistance, and or advice, a competent professional should be consulted. The author specifically disclaims all responsibility for any liability, loss, or risk, personal or otherwise, that is incurred as a consequence, directly or indirectly, of the use and application of any of the contents of this book.

www.xulonpress.com

TABLE OF CONTENTS

Foreward ix
Acknowledgements xi
Taking Inventory 1
   Procrastinating About Not Procrastinating? 1
   Friendly Warning 3
   Reality Check 3
   Procrastination Areas 5
   Round to It 6
   Self Control – Determination - Patience 10
Taking One Thing at a Time 13
   One of "Those" Days? 13
   Rules of the Game 14
   Here Today, Gone Tomorrow! 18
Taking Care of Yourself 23
   Procrastination May be Hazardous to Your Health 23
   Beware of Sharp Edges 26
   Too Busy to Eliminate? 29
   Time or Money 31
Taking Care of Business 33
   Buried Alive in Paperwork! 33
   Gotcha, Insufficient Funds! 34
   Hundred Dollar Movie! 35
   Back to the DMV 36
   Being Late Again? 37

    Phone Calls Anyone? 39
Taking Time to Slow Down 41
    Denial and Self-Deception 41
    Dealing With It..43
    What is Bothering You? 44
    There is an Answer...45
    Someday I am Going to Write a Book!.....................................46
Taking Time to Plan..49
    Cramming for the Test 49
    The Famous Old Waitress 50
    Unchangeable Regrets Due to Procrastination 52
    Planning a Trip? 53
    What Did You Say?...56
Taking Time to Reflect..59
    Cold as Ice..59
    Finish What You Start 63
    The Old Quilt 67
    Some Things Should be Put Off 68
    How Long, How Long? 70
    Aging & Procrastination 71
    The Grand Finale 78

FOREWARD

Brenda Ballantine and I met happenstance years ago and developed an immediate connection. Through her work with burn survivors, I came to know her as an incredibly compassionate and optimistic woman. I would have never described her as a procrastinator. However, over the years I've come to know her as what may be graciously stated as a consummate multi-tasker. I suppose with a mind as active as hers, procrastination is inevitable. Getting it all done is impossible.

In *Pitfalls From Put-Offs*, Brenda writes not as a woman who has it all together and preaches from a lofty height, but as a person who faces the same daily stress as the rest of us and uses the methods described herein to cope and organize her time. Readers will identify with Brenda's real life stories and laugh along with her charming foibles, while at the same time absorbing lessons in life management and spiritual values.

Marilyn Wooley, Ph.D
Clinical Psychologist
Redding, California

ACKNOWLEDGEMENTS

I want to thank a number of people for their help and assistance to bring this book to its final stage. I was encouraged to push through the challenges, pass up temptations to quit, and spurred on when I wanted to put off taking the final steps. Without their love and faith in my ability, and their willingness to share their gifts and talents, I would not have been able to see this completed work. A special thanks to my friends who were there cheering me on all the way to the end of the race.

- I thank God for giving me the ability to write and enjoy this beautiful journey we call life.
- I want to thank my husband Ed for creating "just the right cover" to reveal what a powerful impact put-off's make in our lives.
- I want to thank Renee Perrin for giving me the title of this book, as we talked about all the pitfalls I have fallen into because of put-off's.
- I want to thank my mother "Joy" who inspired me to push past my failures and become all that I can be.
- I want to thank Chris Soares for his willingness to share his knowledge and assist in the process of getting this book published.

- I want to thank all those who read my manuscript and added their own unique perspectives as I wrote and re-wrote the stories within.
- I want to thank all five of my daughters who make life worth it all because of their ability to teach me how to see the world through young and new eyes, full of love and adventure.

Editor : Melissa Hope Gomes
Illustrator : Steve Ferchaud
Cover Design : Ed Ballantine

Taking Inventory 1

*PROCRASTINATING ABOUT NOT
PROCRASTINATING?*

"No pressure" she utters. What does THAT mean? Seriously, when someone wants to make a person panic, they only have to whisper "no pressure" as they quietly exit a room.

Let's take a step out of the "de-pressurized" shoes. Take a quick glance at what physical symptoms happen when someone negates words, with what you know is a falsehood, as soon as it leaves the lips of the fibber.

HOT Flash: Like you have been caught un- prepared on the verge of a conference where you are the key note speaker.

Increased heart rate: Does this count as my daily ration of cardio? Seriously I want to know!

Dry Mouth: Sally Sees Sea Shells Down by the Sea Shore. Does anyone have some water?

Classic Fight or Flight Syndrome: This is all due to a one word experience called "STRESS."

If you find you are the victim of these circumstances maybe a little too often for comfort, then its high time you follow me into this journey. We will explore the life of the procrastinator and all the stress that we create ourselves, for ourselves. Even though you may be in denial, and tell yourself at the last minute "no pressure", we all know we are lying to ourselves, and in truth, WE are the fibbers.

Now I ask you, have you ever bought a book about procrastination and thought you would read it "later"? I have, several times! I often ask myself as I write this book, "Will anyone ever read it"? I know one thing for sure — if I don't finish it, no one ever can!

I wonder how many thousands of authors have written incredible stories... yet they lie in bits and pieces, possibly scattered about, because they did not follow through to the end. It would be a shame after working hard on a book for months, or even years, then procrastinate and not bring it to completion.

There are times when I find it hard to make a commitment to stick with a project until it is finished. I know how I am, and if I get bored, I won't want to work on it anymore. It doesn't matter if it is something hard or easy, if it loses my interest I will want to move on to something more exciting or entertaining. Do you ever feel that way?

The truth is, whether you are building a house, writing a book, or painting a picture, it is not of any value until it is complete. No one likes to read a book without an ending. Whether it is a hammer and a nail, a line in a paragraph, or one stroke of the brush, you are still making progress as long as you don't quit.

Whatever you are attempting to do, if you begin feeling overwhelmed, just tell yourself to "Do the next thing." Remember, we just need to keep moving forward. Some things in life will get in the way of our plans, and then our plans get postponed. That is different than procrastinating.

There will also be times when you need to give yourself permission to rest and regroup at a later date. When things get postponed, we may get disappointed, irritated, or even angry and resentful towards others. Frustrations arise, and then we don't want to do anything and eventually stall out. That is a good time to take inventory of the situation, and then start over with a fresh perspective.

It is important to acknowledge that getting help to address a certain area may also be necessary. The main thing is not to give up while you are in the process of completion. Many times I remind myself, "Success is getting up one more time than you fall down." I confess, I have had many falls and had to get up more times than I would like to admit.

It is important to find a balance and to be able to recognize if we are going in the wrong direction. We must be aware if we are pushing ourselves too hard. If we do end up working ourselves to exhaustion we will lose productivity. This can strain relationships if we do not find balance and rest when needed. If we do not push ourselves enough that raises another issue.

FRIENDLY WARNING

When we decide we are not going to procrastinate any longer, the "Fear of procrastinating" may cause us to over-compensate. Desiring to do everything we can, we lose the ability to enjoy the process of maturing. As you and I continue to move forward with wisdom, we will strike a balance. With this balance, we will be able to do some of the things we procrastinated doing in the past. At other times, we can be content to put things off, knowing it is OK to rest, relax, and enjoy the beauty of the day.

REALITY CHECK

Here is a questionnaire to help you see clearly how much of a procrastinator you really are. The first test will be to see if you will actually pick up a pen and begin answering ten simple questions, or will you decide to do it later? ...You know, when you have more time to "really think" about the answers. On the other hand, maybe you don't feel like getting up to find a pen right now, so you will do it in a little while. Or you could be so excited because you are actually reading this book that you cannot stop now! You can always do it later, right? When you decide you are ready, put everything else on hold for just a few moments, get a pen, and begin your reality check.

- ❏ *Do you put off doing something you do not want to do until later?*

- ❏ *Do you put off making necessary phone calls that you do not want to make?*

- ❏ *Are you late to meetings because you put off going until the last minute?*

- ❏ *Have you lost money due to late fees on bills or overdraft charges at the bank?*

- ❏ *Do you put off getting in shape or exercising until tomorrow?*

- ❏ *Are there jobs that are incomplete because you did not want to finish them?*

- ❏ *Have you put off starting to eat right until next month?*

- ❏ *Have you had any services shut off because you forgot to pay the bill?*

- ❏ *Are you going to get your house in order tomorrow?*

- ❏ *Will you deal with spiritual, emotional, or physical issues later?*

I believe everyone in the human race deals with these issues in some area and this book describes real-life situations. It will also show some of the consequences that are the result of procrastination.

Fear of failure and fear of success can also cause one to delay.

What does it mean to procrastinate? According to some of the world's most trusted dictionaries, the definition of "procrastinate" is, "To defer action; delay, especially intentionally or habitually." Another way of saying "procrastinate" is, "The act of putting something off until a later time." Indecision, or mildly put, not making up your mind, can also cause one to procrastinate. That is, not taking care of business when needed, or not doing things you know you have to do.

Fear of failure and fear of success can also cause one to delay. Distraction also has been a major problem for many. Lost momentum will slow things down to the point where one no longer desires to do anything. Perhaps that is when things just continue to sit on the back burner or bottom shelf.

PROCRASTINATION AREAS

In what areas do you have a tendency to procrastinate the most? In a poll the number one response was in the area of exercise, with eating right coming in second. There are so many areas affected by procrastination that it is difficult to say what is truly number one. When asked the question, "Can you stop procrastinating?" a majority responded, "Yes, if I put my mind to it." A few said they did not know, and some said "No." I believe that we have the tools to make the changes we desire in our lives. Whatever definition of procrastination applies to us individually, it is now possible to make positive changes to begin moving in a new direction.

ROUND TO IT

Have you ever found yourself in the middle of a mindless chore, like doing the dishes, when someone came along and asked you to do something for them? It was not your responsibility, yet they desired to make it yours by handing it off. Mind you, it was one of those "this is not going to be fun" situations that had to be addressed. Actually, it was somewhat important and should have been taken care of several weeks earlier. Although that person just didn't get "around to it", now they want you to be responsible. Perhaps you know about 'Those' kinds of jobs.

Here you are in the middle of your own job, and now one more thing is added on to your to-do list. You say, "OK" but inside you're thinking, "I don't want to do that!" You shelve the thought concerning their request in the back of your mind. Have you ever wondered how big the back of your mind is? It seems I find there is a lot of stuff back there!

The next thing you know, he or she comes in and asks if you have completed the job. Guess what the answer will be. "No!" Did you forget? It could have been because there was so much on the back shelf already that you failed to see it. On the other hand, the thought did keep coming up, "You need to do...." But you put it off because realistically you were not able to do it in the first place. Perhaps you did not think it was that important, or thought that you could do it later.

Other demands may come up that drew your attention away from what you had originally planned to do. The bottom line, you put it off—procrastinated—and now the opportunity for strife has arrived on the scene. Your husband or wife, or whomever you agreed to help, may be thinking you purposely did not do what they asked you to. Was it because you were being irresponsible or did not care about his/her feelings? By thinking it was not important to you even though it was to them, they could become offended.

Among the fruits of procrastination are strife and anger. How can one prevent the above scenario? When someone comes to you and asks you to do something for them, first of all, you need to "pay attention" to their request. Listening is the first step in making sure you clearly hear what they are requesting of you. There have been times that I have looked at my husband and have seen his lips moving, have heard his voice, and even nodded my head obligingly. Then later I realized I was not really listening to him. What did he want? What did he say?

...many fail to see "why" we procrastinate.

To be honest, there were even times when I would say "Yes," and did not really think about the consequences. How much will it cost me? How much time will it take? Do I even have the ability to do any more? I need to stop and take into account what commitments I already have. Desiring to be nice, I would just say, "O.K., I'll do it." Later I realized that I'd have to take care of this and that first; I just couldn't get to his request yet. Unfortunately, I delayed saying that I was over-committed. Pride ("Superwoman to the rescue.") or fear of hurting someone's feelings or disappointing them may have caused me to hesitate addressing these issues many times. After all, I said I would do something but found that I couldn't accomplish the task. I thought I could do it all. Ideas of, "I can handle it." "I will take care of it." "I will fix it." "I…." "I…." "I…." Help! I guess I really am <u>not</u> super woman! What was I thinking?

We can see the results of procrastination in many areas of our lives. Believe it or not, dilatoriness is at work. One might ask me to describe dilatoriness. Actually it is slowness created as a direct consequence of not getting around to it. How many times have things slowed down to a snails pace, or stopped completely when I put them off until the famous, "later"?

What many fail to see is "why" we procrastinate, and what are we going to do about it? There are hundreds of thousands of people in psychological counseling trying to find out the "whys" in their lives. Why do I do this or that? Where the rubber meets the road, or the bottom line, so to speak, is not "why" but "what" are you going to do about it.

It is difficult face the fact that many times we may waver because of fear. You need to ask yourself this question: "Do I want to change?" Are you willing to take a close look at yourself? It may be painful, but it will be profitable. Once you have made the decision that you are ready to change, the process becomes easier.

You are probably thinking, "How can it be easy? I have been a procrastinator my whole life!"

Anyone can begin to change starting the moment the decision is made to do so. This is a scary thought for a procrastinator. The immediate reaction for many is, "Not now, I will make that determination later." I have heard that decision makes a doorway to new realities. That's exciting, yet how many times have I postponed doing what I was suppose to because I was afraid to make a decision? It does not matter if you are the worst procrastinator on planet earth, there is hope and you can stop today. All the procrastination you did from the time you were a little child up and until one minute ago is in the past. Many of the reasons we hesitate are purely habitual. All habits are subject to change when dealt with individually. As you read this book, you will be given ideas and insights. Depending on the choices you make, will determine the degree of your success in breaking the strongholds that procrastination has on your life. The past is gone, and tomorrow is not here yet. Today you can begin all over again.

You will have to count the cost. What is it going to take to change? It could be as low as a measly ten dollars, perhaps one hundred, an astronomical doctor bill, or counseling expenses! What are you willing to pay in time, energy, money, or in other things? The first step is making a decision that you need to change and that procrastination is very costly in many areas. The real question is what price are you already paying?

Scary decisions in the revolving doorway of life.

Loss of time is the most expensive. For we all are allotted a certain amount of minutes, hours, and days on planet earth, and once time is spent we cannot go out and buy more. Loss of health, money, reputation, status, peace, joy, happiness, the list could go on and on. A better question might be: What will it cost if you decide not to change?

Loss of time is the most expensive.

Change can be a scary word. Nevertheless, to get a different outcome, we have to ask ourselves what is required to shift our thinking to bring about different behavior. It will take discipline, determination, self-control, and patience, to begin. These are just a few of the tools you will use as you begin a new life free from the habit of procrastination. With new knowledge, friends' encouragement, others will arise as you continue to grow and change your habits. It is important to apply these principles on a day-to-day basis. Instead of thinking you will get around to it, you will be using self-control to help yourself change the old habit of procrastinating.

If you are like me, the words below are alarming and sound hard to accomplish. I know how I am, and there are times when I just don't want to deal with certain things.

SELF CONTROL – DETERMINATION - PATIENCE

If you and I were exercising self-control, we might not be in some of the messes we are right now. Self-control—what a novel thought! At times, I've wished someone else would come along and just take care of everything. However, the moment I think someone really might be trying to do so, all my alarms go off and I am ready to rumble. So, if I am not willing to let someone else control me, which is good, and if I do not want to be considered "out of control," my only other option is self-control.

Personally, I believe this is only possible with divine help! I get so tired of continually putting things off that are extremely important. Later paying the price, dealing with the problems that have occurred directly related to delays and lack of self-control.

Diligence is a tool that I can use to break the habit of procrastination. I am committed to seeing this habit changed in my life. I do realize that, being human, I will mess up at times, so I am not being totally unrealistic. As I get serious and believe I can succeed, I will make progress toward the desired changes.

I also acknowledge that there are times when what I perceive to be the problem may not be the problem at all. For example, in the human body a pinched nerve in the back may cause pain in the big toe. The cause of procrastination may be something that does not appear to be related—perhaps low self-esteem, fear of failure, acts of self-sabotage, or other hidden agendas.

Determination to find the root cause and deal with it is an inward decision to go forward. Even when all circumstances may appear to be difficult, the rewards are great when one follows through. This is where patience has to come into play. As we move forward toward the goal of freedom from procrastination, let us be patient with ourselves.

The cause of procrastination may be something that does not appear related –

I realize it is human nature to hesitate when it comes to doing something that is not pleasurable, and many times I do that just because I can! Yet reality sets in sooner or later and I find feelings of guilt come flooding in like a tidal wave. Was it worth the cost? Not usually.

Taking One Thing at a Time

ONE OF "THOSE" DAYS?

What happens when you are experiencing "one of those days"? You know, when you feel as if you weigh 2,000 pounds and even breathing seems to require more effort than it's worth. You are not sick; you just don't feel like doing anything. Of course, it seems that "one of those days" always falls on the day that your calendar is chock-full and the to-do list is a mile long.

Here comes the choice. We can pull the covers over our head and stay in bed, or put one foot on the floor and then the other. One step at a time will get you a little further toward your destination or goal. Congratulate yourself. You are up and on the move. Decide that you will be kind to yourself. You need to accept the fact that, in life, there will be times when it is just one of those days. That is when it is good to take time to determine what really is at the top of the priority list, and then just deal with that.

Knowing you might be experiencing "one of those days", decide what you cannot afford to put off until a better time, and address it. Then be sure to give yourself grace concerning those things you need to put on hold. There will be times when it is prudent to shelve something until you are in a better position to accomplish the required task. When you see that is the case, recognize the difference between procrastination and the wisdom to wait.

RULES OF THE GAME

Why is it that I always seem to be running to try to make up for something I didn't do earlier? It seems as if the game has already started, and all the players are on the field fully engaged, and I am still trying to figure out what the rules are. How did I miss that class? When I am in a state of chasing the wind, I ask myself, "What am I doing?" Better yet, "What am I doing wrong? How do I change?"

No matter how I feel, as long as I stay in the game of life, that is what is most important. One hundred years from now, it will not matter how much money was in my bank account, what sort of house I lived in, or what kind of car I drove. Hopefully, I will have made a positive difference in the world. Perhaps I was able to play an important role in the life of a child, a neighbor, a friend, or a co-worker. Whatever I desire to do to make a difference, now is the time to do it.

I heard some one say, "If you don't have time to do it right the first time, when will you?" Being aware of that point of view *now* is the time to accomplish whatever we can. It sounds good, but sometimes we may not want to do our best. Today, for example, I spent hours choosing file cabinets to buy so that I can file papers. I knew I would have to be sorting through specific stuff all day. I was not happy about this idea at all. Not only was it Saturday; it was hard for me to be inside when it was so beautiful and sunny outside. I didn't want to be berating myself, but I was frustrated because of all the piles of paperwork that required my attention.

I called a friend and vented my frustrations. He asked me, "Why is it that your garage is messy?" It took me aback. "What is he talking about?" I wasn't whining about my garage, I'm griping about stupid piles of paper. Actually, it is well known that paper has no intelligence, stupid or otherwise. Have you ever heard yourself saying, "I can't find that stupid piece of paper?" The answer to his question became obvious. It was because I didn't put things back in the garage where they belonged when I was finished with them. In the same way, when dealing with paperwork, I wasn't putting it where it belonged. To have done so would have saved so much time in the end. As I conquer the temptation to keep making piles for the "to be filed" pile, I will be free to enjoy my Saturdays in the sun.

For some people Saturday has a different feel than the rest of the week. I know many celebrate it in a variety of ways. Perhaps it is a day not to do any chores and just rest. I think that is great and welcome the idea. How many are able to do that I don't know.

For others, they go to work from eight to five, Monday through Friday and Saturday is the only day they can sleep in.

My problem is that my puppy does not understand that it is Saturday, as he licks my face and whines, waking me with the desire to get up and play. Puppies can be worse than the kids when it comes to that. Grumbling, I give in and climb out of bed. After leaving the warmth and comfort of my cozy blankets, I have to face the hard realities of the cold floor with my bare feet. Now I am really awake!

Since I am up, I might as well feed all the animals. I can hear the birds singing in their cage, chirping away as the sunrise begins to brighten up the kitchen. I notice that their cage needs some attention, as well as feeding and watering them. Just as I finish taking care of the birds, I hear the cat crying at the front door. Now that it hears that I am up it's not going to quit meowing until I let it in. I thank God that at least the shark in the fish tank doesn't make any noise!

Now it is my turn. Luckily, my husband and kids are not up yet. I have a few minutes of quiet time between the sounds of pets munching their food and everyone else's waking up. "I hope they can sleep in," I think, as thoughts race toward all the things that were put off during the week.

Remember, we are not procrastinating when the reality is that we have a full workload all week and could not possibly complete all the chores around the house.

You look around to see a layer of dust and cobwebs that seemingly magically appeared overnight. Do you ever feel as if some things are completely out of your control, like grass growing three inches in two days? This is not fair; nevertheless, we still have to deal with it. Someone has to mow the lawn, right? We sure don't want the neighbors complaining.

Saturday Morning Blues

Do you ever feel as if some things are completely out of your control...?

What about all those wonderful windows we look through? How do they get so dirty when they are never touched? It's as if we have invisible enemies making messes we have to clean up all the time. If we don't, are we considered "bad house keepers"?

Living on a spinning ball of dirt definitely has its effects on the environment. So why do we have to dust? I do understand the frustration—daddy long leg spiders wanting to set up house keeping in virtually every corner of the house. It seems as if it is a never-ending battle! Now the Saturday Morning Blues have arrived again. My mind continues to go endlessly over all the jobs that need to be done. The to-do list gets longer and longer.

At times we all want to run away and experience something fun instead of having to be responsible and take care of business. When is the last time you took time to fly a kite, have a picnic, or go fishing with friends? I believe it is important to deal with the Saturday Morning Blues which can be accomplished in several ways. In certain ways the adult part of us has to address the need and get the job done. Yet there are times when we all need to just be like a kid again, intentionally putting off those never-ending chores (for a little while) and just enjoy being alive.

HERE TODAY, GONE TOMORROW!

If you think you are going to do something "someday", simply take a close look at your calendar. I see Monday through Sunday, but no "Someday" anywhere on it. Another reality check is the fact this day never returns. When I think about the simple truth that I am in charge of the way I am spending my time, and that today is not coming back, it is a sobering thought. Therefore, the choices I am making at the moment should be respectfully made. I need to be honest and ask myself, how do I want to spend my time? The key words are "want" and "spend".

Sometimes we can spend our time doing things that are fun, yet are they what we want to do?

For example, did I really want to play the piano? I have often thought about how wonderful it would be. Of all the music I listen to, the piano takes me to the heights of ecstasy. I taught myself how to play guitar when I was younger and then later took lessons from a master musician. As time passed I was taught music theory and had lessons to play the bass. I find it interesting hindsight that I would take time to learn these instruments, yet put off learning my true love, which is to have the ability to play piano. The funny thing is when I was a child my parents had a piano. When my father decided to move from the city to the ranch, the piano was moved out to the barn. I remember spending hours out there singing to the cows, and playing to my hearts content. Looking back now I can guess there was more than one reason why the piano was put outside besides the fact they didn't have room for it in the house!

As I write, I realize it still is not too late to learn. All I have to do is make a decision. Do I really want to play, if so, when would I start taking lessons? Am I willing to pay the price, financially as well as making the time commitments?

When will you begin?

Will that be tomorrow? What about that painting class—perhaps tomorrow also? I know I am so tempted to take a break from finishing this book "until tomorrow". It is not easy to be a writer. It is summertime and friends are out having fun and enjoying the beauty of the day. Many times I thought I could wait until later to write, and did, yet the truth is I don't know what tomorrow will bring. So I am choosing to be diligent and to work on this now.

Do you ever think about when tomorrow really starts? It is at 12:01 a.m., technically, but is that when your tomorrow begins? When I say I will do something tomorrow it usually is a vague thought as to when that will occur on my real timetable. I might even say the words, "I will do that tomorrow," although I haven't even thought about what that looks like, or how I will do it. That can lead to another problem, and then the temptation to procrastinate comes up again.

Is life a trial run?
Is this a dress rehearsal?

Recently, I stopped to think about these questions: Is life a trial run? Is this a dress rehearsal? Since it is not, what are we doing with our time? What have we committed to that we may or may not be willing or able to do? Since the reality is that none of us will be here forever, why do we put off doing things we might desire? What belief system causes us to postpone even our own pleasures? This does not mean to be selfish, yet how many of us postpone having fun because we are too busy? Tomorrow we can enjoy…?

Sometimes we get so busy, so caught up in the whirlwind around us, that we lose sight of some of the basics of life. Taking time to care for ourselves is one of those basics I want to discuss. Some people may be afraid to talk about something as sacred as health, nutrition, and exercise. "Oh, that must be one of those health nuts and wacko extremists." How many millions of Americans are suffering because they have put off taking care of themselves in even the simplest ways? What ever happened to eating breakfast? Do we not even have time to sit down and eat because we are in such a big hurry? There are many who grab a quick cup of coffee, perhaps add a muffin or piece of toast, and they are out the door. Children will say, "Mom, I want to get to school early. Can't I eat there?" With no time to put fuel in the body, we use our reserves and then try to hurry through the day. Soon the machine begins to wear down. Constipation sets in, warning signs are flashing yellow lights, yet we still can't slow down. Accidents are just ahead.

Whether people like it or not, the design of our bodies requires that we take care of them. If we do not go by the owner's manual and follow directions, we will not have the performance we desire. In time, with enough abuse, the machine breaks down and will no longer function. But we tell ourselves, "Tomorrow I will change my habits and start feeding myself properly, and I'll exercise!"

Sound familiar? If we want to make real changes we can decide to go outside "today" and walk around the block. If that is too much, try just walking to the corner. Any action made will produce positive results, and you can be proud of yourself while conquering those feelings of discouragement! In addition, you can celebrate the beginning of a new day in a new way.

Taking Care of Yourself

PROCRASTINATION
MAY BE HAZARDOUS TO YOUR HEALTH

Lately, I notice my blue jeans are getting tighter and tighter. It seems as if I keep having to readjust myself as I am pulling things up and pushing things down. Have you ever found yourself sitting at a meeting and soon you feel as if your button is going to pop off your pants? Secretly you try to slip your hand under your shirt and loosen the pressure for temporary relief. You hope that the zipper will not slip too low since you have to readjust everything before anyone sees what you've done. Perhaps you didn't really want to wear those jeans but couldn't find any other clean ones that still fit.

Here is just another reminder that we were going to lose those extra ten pounds starting tomorrow. People say that when you get older you gain weight because your metabolism slows down. That must be the reason I am so tired. Surely, it couldn't be the pizza, lasagna, submarine sandwiches, chips and salsa, or other similar things I have consumed for the last seven years! You know the old saying, "If you keep doing what you're doing you are going to keep getting what you've got?" Well, I've got it! Only ten or fifteen pounds over-weight, but where am I supposed to hide it in these already form-fitting jeans?

I am not hiding anything, everyone can see exactly where my excess is—everyone but me! I don't have eyes in the back of my head but I definitely feel those uncomfortable and extremely tight pants I try to squeeze into. At that time, behavior modification rewards did not seem to motivate me. Money, new clothes, especially a brand new pair of pants (that actually were comfortable and fit well) would be mine if I lost only ten pounds! Yet I continued to grow. So I have decided that I am getting serious now, and tomorrow I am going to start eating right and getting more exercise. Does it sound as if you have heard all this before? It is true. I have lost count of how many times I have said with true intent "Tomorrow...." and then revert back to my old habits.

You know how it goes. Tomorrow is Suzie Q's birthday and, of course, you have to have pizza and soda at the party. What kind of party would it be if we didn't get to eat cake and ice cream to celebrate? A momentary thought might enter my mind about my determination to eat right yet it quickly gets dismissed. After all, it is traditional to indulge for birthdays, right?

Does "celebrate" eventually end up really being spelled "cellulite"?

OK, it is a brand new day. I am really going to start now, and this time I am going to be good. Oh, I almost forgot I was supposed to meet Alice at the Feedbag. That restaurant has the best pancakes in town. We try to meet at least once a month so we can catch up on what is happening with each other's lives. Right after we drop the kids off at school we get together and enjoy time to relax before we have to go to work. My thoughts begin with the idea, maybe I will have that French toast with bacon and eggs instead of pancakes; it will be a nice treat. When I get to work, I get a surprise phone call from a friend, "Can I take you out to lunch at Sheri's?" They have a wonderful chicken fried steak with gravy and baby red potatoes smothered in butter with cooked apples and cinnamon for dessert. How can I say no? I do not want to hurt his feelings. I will just skip dinner and take a long walk. Then I remember my two children at home who like to have something I have heard people call "dinner". For some strange reason they are looking to me to cook. I would still like to see where that unwritten law is hidden that perpetuates the mindset that women are supposed to know "how" to cook. Not only does she know how, she does so with an endearing smile. She has high expectations of loving approval, with oohs and aahs from her loved ones as she sets her masterpiece on the kitchen table for all to admire. They immediately devour all of it, afterward grunt and groan, finally leaving the table with pants unbuttoned for comfort. Then she has the privilege of cleaning the table quickly, washing the dishes sparkling clean and singing praises to God for her wonderful family that she can serve so willingly and happily.

Oh my! I must have slipped into a different world for a moment. It seems to me, at least in my life, that someone was dreaming to come up with those expectations. Yet as bizarre as that seems to me, I think some people have those expectations and get them, others are often highly disappointed. Well, I guess tomorrow I could put on my little apron and begin looking at cookbooks and try to accomplish that goal. For now, let's go out and grab some hamburgers and milk shakes, and share some fries, because tomorrow we start our diet.

BEWARE OF SHARP EDGES

There might be times when we put off something that is absolutely crucial to our own well being. It may seem like a little thing at first, yet if unattended it can become a full-blown tragedy. For the majority, this particular subject is one that most would agree comes with a form of dread attached to it. I must confess that I too am guilty of putting this off as much as possible even though I know better. What is it? Going to the dentist! It's been said that "An ounce of prevention is worth a pound of cure." Yet fear, lack of money, being too busy, and other obstacles can cause us to delay the inevitable.

This is a true story addressing that issue. While working together with a gentleman on a major project, I noticed he was not acting like he normally did. He began complaining about a tooth that was bothering him. Apparently the filling had fallen out, and he had not gone to the dentist to deal with it. When it first happened, he couldn't get it fixed because he was sick. Then he didn't have money for an appointment. Once he had finances to go, he was too busy. As you might have guessed he didn't want to deal with it. He continued dragging his feet as the clock kept ticking away.

The problem was that a sharp edge on the tooth began irritating his tongue. He tried to ignore it, but the pain continued to increase as the damage was being done. As his friends we would ask him to go to the dentist and get help to relieve his suffering.

He would say, "Yeah, I know I need to go to the dentist but...." And he still put it off. He was really busy, like many of us, and he didn't want to take the extra time to deal with the problem. Other circumstances continued to arise, adding to the delay. His tongue was in so much pain that he was no longer able to eat normal food. He was so busy working that his wife would have to bring him soft foods to the office that he could just swallow. Concern, uncertainty and fear began to arise as his friends and family saw him begin to lose weight from not being able to eat.

He finally decided to stop putting off making the appointment, face his fears, spend the money, and see a dentist. After grinding the sharp edge and making it smooth, the dentist said he needed to refer him to an oral surgeon because of the way his tongue looked. The oral surgeon immediately took a biopsy. In the meantime, the pain of chewing food grew so intense that he could barely eat. He continued to lose weight. By the time the results came back from the test he had already lost 20 pounds. Confirming everyone's fear; he was diagnosed with cancer of the tongue. The surgeon said he would have to cut half of his tongue out, remove his saliva glands, and take out all of the lymph nodes in his neck.

The circumstances that began to evolve were financially astronomical and emotionally exhausting. He kept shaking his head in disbelief saying, "If only I hadn't put off taking care of that tooth, none of this would be happening now." Over and over he repeated himself, if only......

His wife's concern about her husband's well being was number one. Yet other thoughts bombarded her mind. How would they survive financially if he couldn't work? Any time someone has to go into the hospital it is costly. Chemotherapy, surgery, and radiation—none of it is cheap. Their sons were also effected by their father's unwillingness to take care of himself, and could have been wondering what they will do in the future. After all, dad has always been there to take care of their needs!

***Putting off basic good
health care is costly,
one way or the other.***

As I tell this story I can ask if this motivated anyone to pick up the phone and make their own dentist appointment. It served to wake me up to take inventory of my own life and that of my family. When was the last time I went to the dentist or the doctor for a check up? Of course, as the procrastinator that I am, after giving it serious thought I decided I would call tomorrow. I can tell you that tomorrow is not the correct answer, yet is an honest one.

It is interesting that we can fail to understand the importance of our own oral health, possibly putting off simple things like flossing our teeth. Later we may find ourselves dealing with circumstances that are not pleasurable, to say the least. Experiencing the loss of teeth, disease, or just bad breath, are all things that we can prevent with proper care—if we do not put it off. In this man's case, he could have prevented physical, emotional and financial loss.

Seeing this happen to a friend should wake us up. With his permission, I decided to share this story in hope that it will remind all of us to take care of ourselves now. All my friend could say over and over was, "If only I had taken care of myself then, none of this would be happening now." This man did not smoke or chew. He just put off going to the dentist to take care of a problem that would literally have taken very little time to remedy. Nevertheless, many began praying for him and his family. The good news is that he successfully went through all of his Radiation and Chemo treatments, did not have to have the surgery to remove his tongue, and is now enjoying his life cancer free.

Sometimes we have to take the time and money to take care of ourselves! If we do not do it now, how much more will it cost us in the future?

TOO BUSY TO ELIMINATE?

Have you ever been constipated with the cares of life? Are you in a hurry to jump back on the freeway of life, racing with all the others on a mission? We may be going to a meeting, work, school, shopping, or church, yet it seems most are in a hurry these days. Wherever you are on earth as you travel in life, you will find that there are those who are rushing to get somewhere hoping they will not be late. We might know logically that if we leave earlier for our destination we arrive early or at least on time. One young man shared with me his thoughts: "If I arrive early, I am on time. I if arrive on time, I am late." With increased population traffic congestion also increases, stress levels rise, as well as all the distractions that come with it.

Blowout on the Freeway of Life

Once we have entered the six-lane freeway traveling seventy miles an hour, do we dare take an exit? Sometimes we need to pull over to see where we are headed. Are we going in the right direction? Where is the map of life that shows the way? Actually, it would have been a lot easier to know the way in the first place. I remember one time when I was driving down the freeway, not knowing where I was, thinking, "I need to pull over and look at the map later, you know, when I stop somewhere to get gas!" Those are the times I know God watches over me.

Sometimes it is important just to get in the slow lane and let everyone pass you by. At other times, we all will need to stop completely. This is where we talk about the nitty-gritty in life. Elimination! Where do we go when we need to eliminate all the excess weights accumulated on the journey? As strange as it may seem for this topic to be in a book about procrastination, it is actually one of the most important aspects of staying healthy. All creation needs to eliminate unnecessary things in one way or another. In science class it is taught that a snake molts, having a whole layer of skin removed. At least we do not have to go that far! Nevertheless, if the process of elimination is put off when nature calls, one can experience many additional difficulties. Yet, at the most humbling and relieving moments, we can still get so caught up in the busyness of life that we may even try to put that off! I realize that some who read this particular section might be thinking, "What? How dare she?"

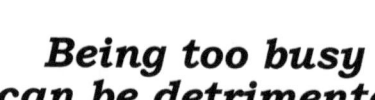

Being too busy can be detrimental to your health.

All things in life need to be balanced, and being in a hurry a majority of the time can lead to serious health issues, as well as other significant problems. Being too busy can be detrimental to your health. As we all continue on this journey, we will learn how to balance our lives in the essentials as well as the non-essentials. Peace of mind comes when we know what we can truly eliminate without having to feel guilty.

TIME OR MONEY

Which is more valuable, your time or your money? The great comedian, Jack Benny, told a story about being held up by a crook who said, "Your money or your life" after a long pause, prompted again by the robber, "Your money or your life" Jack replied..... I'm thinking, I'm thinking! Many laughed at that old joke, yet it is true, we have to ask ourselves the same question. If we only have a limited amount of money, with no possibility of getting more, would we arbitrarily spend portions of it, sometimes small amounts, sometimes large? We also understand we only have so much time, we have a limit and that is all we will get. Once it is spent, it is gone for good.

We can't reverse the clock and get back even one second. When we are young we may not really comprehend the reality of that limitation. Why? When it comes to money, we can try to find a way to get more somehow when we really need it, even if we had to borrow it. Yet when it comes to time, we can not add one extra minute. As I stated before, this day never returns, but you do get to choose how you spend it.

Now we have to understand that as things change we need to be wise, we need to use discretion when spending our substance. In this same way, we need to see that we have been given time, the divine gift of life, and yet it also is apportioned in a limited amount. Once time is spent, it has been spent forever. How you decide to spend it is up to you.

When you procrastinate, many times you will end up having to spend minutes or hours trying to find something, or fix something, that you postponed dealing with earlier. How many days are spent looking for that important document because you failed to put it in its proper place? How much time was spent looking for a tool lost in the stuff packed into the garage that will be cleaned "tomorrow"? Remember that each time we are tempted to put something off; it will probably cost us something later. Speaking from my own experience, I can see how I foolishly spent precious time "needlessly" because I didn't pay attention. Although there is no condemnation, it is a reality I need to see so that I am willing to make changes. The truth is I can not change history, but I can change the future by making good choices now.

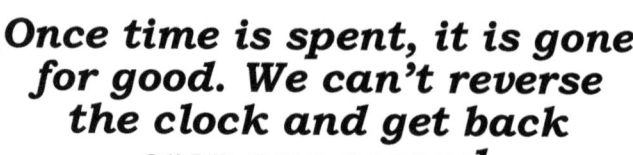

Once time is spent, it is gone for good. We can't reverse the clock and get back even one second.

Taking Care of Business

BURIED ALIVE IN PAPERWORK!

Do you ever feel as if you are being buried alive in paperwork? Have you ever had the thought, "I need to file these documents, but I don't have time to right now?" What do you do? Do you simply set them down on the table "for now"? Warning! The next day more papers will come in. (We have become a paper-driven society.) Have you ever noticed how much paperwork there is? It is everywhere you go. We get all kinds of receipts for this and that. Bills and junk mail arrive, faithfully delivered by our wonderful postal service. Even if you go to the DMV, they will ask you to fill out papers, please. It seems as if everywhere you go, there is a paper trail following you.

I do realize that there are those absolutely unique people who are organized and love paperwork. They thrive on organizing it all. They not only love it, they deal with it as soon as they encounter it. Then there are those of us who have the "to be filed pile", dating back to the '60s. Sometimes we do actually sort through some of the papers and throw out the trash. Yet the other pile keeps growing and

growing. What is the reason? Procrastination? The thought process may be something like this, "I don't have enough time to do all this right now, so I will do it later." Or, "It will take too long to finish, so tomorrow I will set up the time to get it done. So the piles just keep getting higher and higher.

The next thing you know, the unfriendly bill collector calls and inquires about a late payment. You state, "That bill was paid, and I have the receipt to prove it!" The person on the line requests a copy to verify your claim. You know it's in the house somewhere. The familiar feeling of frustration arises again, all because it was not filed in the proper place. The temptation to become angry grows as time is spent trying to find it.

Feelings of anxiousness begin to spring up as you wonder where it could be. You ask yourself if you will ever find it. Two hours later, you finally find it and a sense of joy and relief momentarily fills your soul. You tell yourself you really need to take time to deal with all that paperwork. You promise yourself you will file later; you can't now, after all, because you just wasted the last two hours looking for that stupid receipt. The next thing you do is throw all the papers back into a box to be filed tomorrow.

GOTCHA, INSUFFICIENT FUNDS!

Have you ever opened the mailbox and found one of "those" envelopes from the bank that make your stomach sink? If you are one of the fortunate ones who do not understand what I am talking about, you should be proud of yourself. If you are like many of us, you would understand probably more than you would like to admit.

Here is a story that reveals why it is bad to procrastinate in areas that are very important. Banking is one of them. One case scenario:

HUNDRED DOLLAR MOVIE!

There are giant red boxes out in front of grocery stores and other prominent locations from which people can rent movies for a dollar each. They are so convenient and easy to use. All you have to do is touch the screen, find a movie you would like to watch, slide your credit card or debit card through, and *voila!*, entertainment for the night! If you want to do a double feature, splurge for two bucks. Now, if you fail to turn them back in the following day, your card will be charged repeatedly—up to twenty-five dollars! Of course, most of us would not fall into that trap, and we do our best to return the movies when we are finished. Here, in this scenario, it was not renting the DVD that was the problem. It was the failure to balance the checkbook, adding the two dollars and fifteen cents that was taken out of the bank account with the debit card. Putting off the simple action of entering a transaction is what caused a domino effect ending up with more than one hundred dollars in bank charges. Banks will admit that they make a large percentage of their income from incidents like this, and they like it when someone, mistakenly or on purpose, overdraws their account.

I do not know how many times I have thought about creating a budget and sitting down at the computer, "tomorrow", to learn the financial program I have installed. With the economy the way it is, and challenging financial times, this should be on my priority list. Next weekend I will set up a time dedicated just to that—right after I finish my shopping!

BACK TO THE DMV

Today, I decided I would make the trip to the Department of Motor Vehicles and get my car registered. First, I would get the car smogged, and enjoy having breakfast (while still on my diet) with a friend. "After all," I thought, "I might as well make this as painless as possible." Finally, it was time to pick up my car. I had such a beautiful day planned. I'd get the car smogged, go to the DMV and register it, do a few errands, and then go to work.

Much to my surprise when I went to pick up the car the woman said, "Your car failed its smog test"! I was caught totally off guard. What? I just came from the mechanic. After spending $240 on car parts, and $160 for two hours of labor, plus the money for a smog test, I still can't register the car?

My plans had now changed. I had to decide what I was going to do. I was so angry I wanted to say, "Forget it, I'll take care of it later." At that very moment, I caught myself. I had a choice. "I can deal with it now, or put it off until later." The circumstances could only get worse from this point. I could forget to do it later and then be pulled over by a police officer for not having the expensive little sticker they so love to see on my license plate, and get a $5,000 fine! I could also pay the DMV even more money later for not paying the registration fee on time.

On the other hand, I could be responsible, even if I was angry, and take care of it. I decided to face my fear of the unknown and act like a grown-up and drive to the DMV. As I waited in line, I wrote this part of this book! It feels so good to be taking care of business. I got a temporary permit taped on the window and off I went. "Now I am free to enjoy the rest of a beautiful day. Tomorrow I will deal with the mechanic!"

BEING LATE AGAIN?

Trying not to procrastinate on yet another thing, here I am standing in the DMV line for the second time today. Looking at the long line of people, young and old, I wonder how many are here at 4:46 p.m. on the last day to register their car or renew their driver's license. How much more will they have to pay because they were late paying their annual dues?

Recently I received a letter in the mail from my bank stating their concern about the lack of insurance on my car. It is amazing how the insurance companies tell the DMV if you are not insured, then they tell the bank, and the bank is quick to let you know there is a problem. I am not one who tries to cheat the system, and that is exactly what it is, but I really didn't know what they talking about? There must be some mistake. I called my agent to find out that the bank was correct! My insurance had been cancelled due to the lack of a payment. It doesn't matter if you have been a faithful customer for thirty five years and pay big payments for three cars and motorcycles, one slip up and your throat is cut, you are out of here, too bad so sad. There is no family ties, no farewell party, not even a friendly note to ask if there is a problem. No....it is just plain and simple, give us your money or else!

How could this be happening? I found the receipt, (a small miracle in itself) and there it was, proof I paid one hundred and twenty dollars...Oh no, that was for the membership dues? How embarrassing! Now I have to go to the insurance company, wait for the agent to assist me, and spend time re-writing our policy. When time is so precious, it is frustrating to have to go back and take care of something that was already done before. This is one more example of the consequences that can take place if I am not paying attention to details. When I delay balancing the check book, or do not pay my bills correctly, I find it usually robs me of more time and money in the future. Although I have a very friendly agent, he too was affected by my mistake. When I called to make an appointment I added one more thing on to his to-do list. I could hear in his voice he was not really excited when I told him the news.

Sometimes things happen that we can't see that are directly related to dilly-dally. In this case, I had a windshield replaced on my Crown Victoria. When they installed it, I noticed there was something wrong with the glass. I travel continually and did not have time to address it at the moment. To be honest, I really didn't want to deal with any confrontation, so I hesitated to say anything. The problem was unique. During the day everything looked fine. But when the windshield got cold and wet, especially at night, (as it does in the winter when it's raining) it was almost impossible to see through. There was some kind of flaw in the glass that was in between the layers so I could not wash it and make it clear. The reason I added this story is because I knew there was a problem with the windshield, yet I delayed addressing the issue. This situation really got my attention when I was driving in a city, 130 miles from home, and it was pouring down rain and dark. Literally I barely could see through the glass. There was no way I was going to be able to drive home. Fear gripped my heart, as I prayed for safety to get to the nearest hotel. As you might guess, it was not cheap. Here is another costly experience that was directly related to dilatoriness.

So how do I keep finding myself in these situations? Even though I am aware of the pitfalls I find myself in, I still am human and make mistakes.

I truly believe we can make changes, big or small, as we become aware of circumstances that have led us in a certain direction.

...the answer comes from within, as we decide to make the right choices and take care of what is at hand.

Have you ever thought about the fact being late and procrastination seem to go hand-in-hand. I find it ironic how many interruptions happened while I was in the process of completing this book. I have a deadline from the publisher today, but I still have to work on the last chapter! After all, how can I finish a book on the topic of procrastination?

Some ask, "Is there a special formula we can use to quit procrastinating?" How about a liquid preparation that may be applied directly to the skin? Maybe someone can invent a "healthy" procrastinator's prescription that has no side effects! What about some special drink that turns peoples' hands bright purple when they procrastinate?

No, I think the answer comes from within, as we decide to make the right choices and take care of what is at hand.

PHONE CALLS ANYONE?

Have you ever had to make a phone call you really didn't want to make? Many times, when I do not want to upset other people, I find myself upset, thinking about upsetting them. I know that sounds strange, yet it is true. So I will delay making the call, and by doing so, make them even more upset!

This can be true when dealing with family members, co-workers, bill collectors or any number of other situations. Ever find yourself secretly hoping that when you do call that they won't answer the phone? That makes it easier because then you can just leave a message? That still delays the process, yet somehow it feels better. What about sending a text, will that work?

Once I get the courage or make the determination to pick up the phone, the next challenge begins. This really bothers me. Who would have ever dreamed we would arrive to the place where we get excited if we actually get to talk to a real human being on the phone. (If you speak English push #1) Oh Please, Help me Jesus! My fingers, as well as my patience, are strained by the time I have pushed so many buttons trying to answer some robot prompting machine.

Don't you love it? Knowing that this is a possibility we have to face in this new world of technology, it is another reason to be tempted to hesitate making a call. It really can take "too" long. We can always do it later; after all, we are busy!

Another fascinating scenario that can happen now is to answer the phone early Saturday or Sunday morning and hear someone from another country trying to pronounce my name in English. Then I get to spend the next ten minutes trying to explain to them there is some mistake, I do not owe seven trillion dollars to guitar center from an unknown transaction back in 1902!

Dreaded phone calls can be about all kinds of issues. One that I dealt with concerned a furniture store. I had ordered a coffee table, end table, and new lamps from a very reputable and expensive store. When the furniture arrived, the door would not open on the end table, the lampshade was flawed and the beautiful coffee table had chunks of wood missing. After ordering new ones and waiting two more months, the replacements too were damaged. I needed to call and deal with it. I had to complain. Sometimes we have to wait until the store opens to call but the question is; how do you handle it? When you remember later you still have to deal with the situation, do you put it off or do you just go for it?

Here is another scenario. Has anyone ever worked on your car, and, when the work was finished, charged you more than you were quoted? To top it off, they demand that you pay or you will not get your keys back! Once you get home, you realize that your car runs worse than it did before it was worked on. What do you do? Will you make the dreaded call, deal with the conflict you know will come, and demand that they fix it? Or, do you think it is better to do it later? After all, you are too upset and too busy right now.

It is hard to confront situations at times, yet it is harder when we put off things that need to be dealt with. Whatever the circumstances, sometimes the call just has to be made. When you hang up, take a moment to acknowledge your diligence and embrace the moment of victory.

Taking Time to Slow Down

DENIAL AND SELF-DECEPTION

How is it that we can be so easily deceived? Have you ever had someone try to rip you off, but they were so obvious that you just shook your head and said, "No way!"? Perhaps a salesperson was racking up the price of an item much more than it was worth. But what if an individual was so sly, so clever, that somehow they got past your guard and you found out too late that you were had? Your response could be anger, sadness, or perhaps indignation.

What is even worse is when you find out that you were the one who deceived yourself. How can that be? What do you mean? I would never.... How many times have you heard yourself say, "I knew I shouldn't have done that? Something inside me was telling me, 'Don't do that.' Yet, as you find yourself kicking your own rear-end, you say, "I won't do that again." What happened? How do you keep falling into that trap? Believe it or not, procrastination is probably working behind the scenes.

If you see yourself stalling instead of taking care of business there should be a warning sign; danger lies ahead. If you chose to delay responding to the signals, the next thing you know, consequences from the bad choice start showing up. Let the games begin! Once you are in, the pieces are all on the board and you find yourself so involved in the game you forget that there ever was any warning. Of course, the game was fixed, similar to those in all the casinos. Perhaps you fell headlong into it for a period of time, and then suddenly reality hits. Maybe you lost all your money, find yourself going through a divorce, or have lost your job.

Sometimes, wake-up calls are Extremely loud.

You ask yourself, "What happened?" "How did I get here?" As you look back, if you will be honest with yourself, you will find that you truly deceived yourself by procrastinating. Not heeding the warning signs from within, or justifying putting off responding to that inner voice, can lead to self-deception and then denial. When we do not do what was needed in the first place, even in some of the simplest things, can lead all of us in a direction we may not want to go.

This is why it is important that when we are first made aware of any thoughts that are "red flags", we need to heed the warning signs, like those on the freeway saying, "Wrong Way - Do Not Enter." No one can change the past. But knowing that procrastination is one of the failings that can trap us into self-deception, we can begin to recognize problems ahead of time and choose to prevent future deceptions. Our freedom is directly related to the choices we make, and to our decisions to act correctly, in a timely matter, in any given situation.

DEALING WITH IT

Have you ever noticed that you begin to feel anxiety because you know that you need to take care of something? Do you hesitate because you don't want to deal with it at the moment? It is not anything difficult (you don't have to dig a ditch), but you just do not feel like addressing the situation right then. It is too easy to just put it off, just for now of course. Each time that nagging thought comes across your mind; you sense that familiar feeling of apprehension. Yet, you still do not want to deal with the problem at hand, so you busy yourself with something else. Soon, you find yourself so stressed out, because you know what you should do. And then you start to feel angry, because you know you really don't want to do what needs to be done. It can be something as easy as taking out the garbage, but you don't want to deal with it "right now".

On a more serious note, sometimes we find ourselves in a frame of mind in which we may even look around for others to blame. For some reason we are angry; it must be "their fault". "Surely, they could have taken care of the situation."

Soon, resentment toward that individual may enter the picture. "After all," we may think, "why do I have to take care of everything?" Peace of mind has disappeared completely. Each time the thought of, "You need to take care of such and such," comes to mind, the feelings of anxiousness, resentment, fear, or guilt rush in. Not wanting to keep experiencing those feelings, we suppress any thoughts about the situation.

But, the more we try to distance ourselves from situations that could bring up those negative feelings; we find it is very difficult to do. I have found that it is much easier simply to attend to circumstances as they arise. Avoidance generally leads to pain and other distressing consequences that — I can guarantee — somehow will always return, sooner or later.

WHAT IS BOTHERING YOU?

Are there things that in your life that bother you? If so, when they do, ask yourself, what do you do about it? I believe we all make decisions when something is bothering us one way or the other. At what point are we willing to make a change? The question is; are we willing to leave things the way they are and just accept them as fate? Or are we willing to pay the price it takes to make a change?

In my life, I keep telling myself that I want to change, but then I end up doing the same thing over again and again. I need to make a choice. Do I leave things status quo? Or, do I remove myself from the circumstances that are influencing me not to make changes? Am I willing to do what it takes? That seems too simplistic to say, but it is accurate. The expression "If you keep doing what you're doing, you're going to get what you got" holds true. If you want something you've never had, you have to do something you've never done.

I don't want to stay with the status quo, if it is destructive to my health, my relationships, or my occupation. I want to work to change the circumstances. I know that is easier said than done, and at times I'm not sure I really even mean it. My actions are louder than my words. Let's take my health for example: I know that I am now overweight. It bothers me. I would like to blame menopause, stress, lack of sleep, etc., but ultimately I am still the responsible one. Yet I do not make the changes needed to get the desired results. I can pray for a slim and trim body until I'm blue in the face. But it will not get me anywhere. Actions bring results. Yes, tight pants make me very uncomfortable. They definitely put a dent in my self-esteem. Yet I delay going to the gym, but just today, tomorrow I go early, first thing in the morning!

It bothers me to feel uncomfortable, yet what do I do to change? When does it get to the point that I am really willing to do something different? As I sit here tonight working on my book I have just finished eating some Chinese fast food! I never go through the drive thru! What was I thinking? What have I done? I must stop sabotaging myself! How many of us have said that? I have a plan! I'm very reward-motivated. Tomorrow I'm going to the store and buy some colorful smiley face stickers to put on my calendar for every day I exercise. When I get 30 stickers in a row I get a reward. Something that is not food-related of course. Something like a nice top or other desired piece of clothing. That will surely motivate me to change. Soon my self-esteem will be improved, and instead of putting off exercise, I can put off putting on tight pants! I will enjoy the freedom of having one less thing bothering me. What is bothering you? You too can make a decision for change.

THERE IS AN ANSWER

In order to change any well ingrained habit, we must recognize the thoughts that motivate the undesirable behavior, and actively redirect those thoughts. When we get into the habit of putting things off, we may not realize why we are doing it. I suspect that the majority of the procrastinator's challenges may have originated when they were very young.

I was the fifth of six girls in my family. There were no boys. We were all born in the city. But my father decided that was not the place to raise young ladies, so he moved us to a dairy farm. My mother would wake me up at four o'clock in the morning to round the cows up and get them into the barn. After the cows were milked, and the barn cleaned, I had to get ready for school. I was always hurrying to get my dress ironed (We had to wear them in the old days!) while I could see the school bus coming down the road. I knew I had to go school every day, yet I would not or could not decide what I was going to wear until the last minute. I must have known I was not going to go naked, nor was I going to wear my pajamas, because I eventually did get dressed! Even to this day, I will find myself in the same dilemma, putting off making the decision of what to wear. As simple as that sounds, it can have a devastating effect on someone when they end up being chronically late to appointments.

...when things are not exciting, fun, or pleasant, it is human nature to put things off.

How many students know all week there will be a test on Friday, and wait until eight forty-five the night before to start studying? Why do they do that? For one reason: when things are not exciting, fun, or pleasant, it is human nature to put things off.

When we know we will be expected to do something, or there will be dire consequences—bad grades, loss of job, etc., some will put off taking care of business as long as possible. One example is waiting until April 15 to pay taxes. The stress of knowing you have to fill out those awful papers and maybe even make a mistake strikes fear in one's heart. Maybe it will be easier later, maybe someone can help! ...All along knowing what has to be done as thoughts keep invading the back of your mind ("IRS...IRS...IRS..."). I do not know anyone who likes to pay taxes. When we stop procrastinating and just get it done, it feels better to be free of one more nagging burden weighing on our shoulders.

SOMEDAY I AM GOING TO WRITE A BOOK!

How many people think they would like to write a book? If you listen to people talk you may hear someone say, "Yeah, I ought to write a book about that." Or, "That would make a great book." Some people think their life story would make a good book. Yet why don't more people write? "Someday, when I get older and can retire, I am going to write a novel!" So the key here is, "someday". Time slips away, and the story disappears, never to be heard. I heard someone say that their story would be like tears in the rain, no one ever really sees them. Knowing that there is not really a "someday" on our calendar, let's pretend that it actually has arrived. You get a pencil and paper, and find a quiet place to begin your journey. You ask yourself a single question.

"What shall I name my book? The title is....? Oh, I will think about that later." The pencil is laid down and off you go to visit a friend! Another story is lost in the pitfall of a put-off. I hope that doesn't happen with yours.

Taking Time to Plan

CRAMMING FOR THE TEST

Imagine being a sixteen-year-old sitting in a science class, daydreaming. Your teacher's lectures are guaranteed to get you nodding off at least a few minutes before he is finished. So you try to look out the window to keep awake. Your mind wanders as you find yourself thinking about the sunshine outside while you are stuck inside. Thoughts of a picnic and lying in the grass are now making your stomach growl.

What did he say? Was the teacher saying something about a test? Tomorrow? With this instructor, the likelihood that a test will be given is almost a sure bet. You decide you had better start paying attention.

For teenagers it is easy to get in the habit of not paying attention, procrastinating about getting homework finished, or of putting off studying for a test. The wake-up call is when they find themselves cramming the night before the exam. Procrastination can be expensive. A bad grade could affect a grade point average. The chance of losing a scholarship for college, of getting kicked off the football team, or of being grounded, all could be other consequences, other manifestations of the pitfalls from put-offs. How many times have we crammed for a test and wondered why we waited so long to prepare beforehand? Were we not paying attention to what was being taught earlier? Sometimes it is not profitable to ignore instructors in our own personal classroom of life.

THE FAMOUS OLD WAITRESS

This morning I was sitting in a popular restaurant, waiting for a client to join me for breakfast. An elderly woman approached me to see if I would like to order anything. She was polite as I explained to her that I was waiting for someone. As I looked at her face, I could see deeply etched lines and wrinkles. Her smile had faded and there was no sparkle in her eyes. Although she had put her hair up nicely, the gray in it told me she was up in years. I observed her movements as she went from table to table, waiting on the customers. I could see her hands tremble as she carried out several drinks and heavy plates full of food. Even though it was early morning, she looked as tired as if she had already put in a full day's work. I figured she must not have any other skills to rely on. Maybe her husband had passed away and she found herself alone, with no one to support her.

How many of us thought that we never had to worry about going to school and getting a job? "After all," perhaps you thought, "I am a wife and mother, and that in itself is a full-time job." Eventually, though, the children grow up and go out on their own. Maybe you have experienced a divorce, or the death of a loved one. Suddenly a different reality sets in. The bills come due, and the need for money—for food and other necessities, as well as entertainment—becomes urgent.

So, out into the job market jungle you go. At every corner, you hear the same request, "May we see your portfolio?" "What level of education did you complete?" Words of the past come flooding in on you. Perhaps it was the wise words of your parents, saying how important it is to get a good education. "You need to decide what career you would like to have." Could it be that those thoughts about your education were pushed aside? After all, you thought, "It is just time to have some fun now."

"Later I'll decide what I want to do." Time keeps rolling on.

Perhaps you had thoughts like, "I'll decide what I want to do, later." Time keeps rolling on. Relationships and an easy part-time job started the ball rolling down hill. The next thing you knew you were married, had gotten old, and now you find yourself asking, "How did I get into this mess? I have no education!" Yes, that is true, and the reason behind it is, once again, "procrastination"—not making the decision as to what you wanted to do, and putting off making the commitment needed a long time ago.

The saying, "I do not know what I want to do when I grow up," may be said even when we find we are getting older. One thing is for sure. Today can be the start of a new beginning. Today we can begin a new part of our education, avoiding the pitfalls from put-offs.

UNCHANGEABLE REGRETS
DUE TO PROCRASTINATION

When I asked a group of women about any thoughts they might have concerning procrastination, I was surprised to hear the response of one young woman who stated that her biggest regret about procrastination was not buying a camera! At first, I thought about all the digital cameras we see sold everywhere these days. I asked her what she meant. It was then that I saw a sadness come over her face. She said, "I kept putting off going to the store and buying a camera. Now I have no pictures of my only child when he was a little boy." It was a tragic moment, in the sense that I could feel her pain. I knew there were no fixes. She could not go back in time, and I had no way to comfort her.

...some opportunities are available only for a limited amount of time on our calendars.

It is true that there are all types of seasons in life. Sometimes we may not be aware of the fact that some opportunities are available only for a limited amount of time on our calendars. The good news in this particular story is that the grandmother of her child and the woman's older sister overheard our conversation. They decided to gather all the pictures of her son they could find from the rest of the family, make copies, and surprise the mom with a photo album. It was filled with awesome pictures of wonderful memories for her to enjoy into her later years. She was saved from one of the pitfalls of put-offs. It is good to know that once in awhile there can be a happy conclusion!

Pitfalls From Put-Off's

PLANNING A TRIP?

Let's say you have just been informed that you have to go on a business trip. Or, possibly a family member has fallen ill and you must go to be of assistance. You've just been notified, and you have to be away for a week. All expenses will be taken care of. All you have to do is prepare yourself and take care of your family's needs.

Here is the scenario: you have a husband, kids, two dogs, birds, and fish. The first thing you have to do is find sitters for the kids. It would be best to farm them out separately so that it will not be too much of a burden on someone. Doing that is not something you can wait until the last minute to do—especially since they will need to be taken to school and picked up each day. Your husband will be going with you. He will have the privilege of preparing his own belongings! I guess that means you cannot leave the laundry until you get back. After all, you are sure he will want clean socks and underwear on the trip. You secure friends to feed the dogs, the cat, the birds, and the fish. You are hoping your wonderful 110-pound German shepherd pup does not break the neighbor's fence again and chew up her new mop. (Remember, the one you had to replace last week?)

Now, it looks as if all the bases are covered. People are taking care of the kids, watching the house, and feeding the animals. You know you have to pack, and you have already made reservations for a rental car. Your goal is to leave by noon. The night before your departure you find yourself dinking around, doing other things. When you finally realize it is so late, you are too tired to do any more, so you tell yourself, "I can pack in the morning."

...not only does my procrastination affect another's life, other people's procrastination affects my life.

You drop the kids off at school, go to the bank, get the rental car, grab something to eat, and finally are back home. Well, the next thing you know the day is half over. The laundry is drying, and your husband is pacing the floor ready to go. Of course, you want something to do while traveling in the car for hours and hours, so you get some sewing materials out. As you start cutting squares of material for the handmade quilt you want to work on in the car you think, "I might as well watch the movie I rented while I work!" Sound crazy? Not only was *I* guilty of not packing the night before, my boss also procrastinated. I had to wait for *his* materials to get back from the print shop before I could leave town. The moral of the story is: not only does my procrastination affect another's life, other people's procrastination affects my life. It ended up that we left four and half hours later than planned. This kept us on the road late at night. Unfortunately, this made it difficult to quilt in the dark. It is frustrating when you get a late start, because you end up trying to play catch-up. Everything is thrown off schedule.

If you look closely at this picture you can see that because I put something off earlier, it had a direct impact on our departure time. Realistically, there are times when circumstances beyond our control keep us from accomplishing our goals. At those times, we just have to accept the things that we cannot change. Everyone has to deal with circumstances like that now and then. However, I am specifically addressing the situation when we may be planning a trip, a journey, an adventure, or a great family vacation. If we want to have a good time, and cut out some potential problems, preparation is the key.

What I mean here is to make a plan and stick with it. Set small goals that are achievable, and then put some action toward the desired outcome, even if the task is something that may seem minor, such as packing an overnight bag. The better we are prepared, the less hassle there will be later. It is important to determine not to put off making arrangements as early as possible. Writing down your plans first will help to begin the process. Then decide what you will need to accomplish to fulfill each part of that plan. Remember, whatever step you take is a victory over procrastination.

Sometimes people do not want to make plans and think them through, because of fear—not having enough money, or enough time, or enough energy. If we do not take time to count the cost (thinking, "I can do it later."), this could hinder our ability to continue. Others, while racing here and there, can actually find themselves running headlong into problems. Without proper planning they quickly find out they are out of gas, or cash and they return home disappointed, angry, or frustrated.

There are times that we do not want to face the fact that we have limitations as human beings. As long as we can procrastinate, even in making plans for something enjoyable, we can stay in our dreamland or fantasy world and not have to be responsible. When I went to Disneyland as a child, I had fun. I was entertained. And by the end of the day, I had a place to sleep. I didn't need to be concerned about financial matters—the cost of my room, how much my tickets were, or how much money they wanted for my hotdog and coke. Adults are the ones who have to be responsible for all that! It would be sad to drive across the United States to Florida and find yourself at the gates of Disney World, only to learn you did not bring enough money to get in. Knowing in advance what it will entail, and being prepared for a trip or a vacation, will help make it enjoyable for all those involved.

Procrastinators who do not want to deal with the responsibilities of adulthood, who want to be the child going to Disneyland, may wake up half way there and realize that their mommy and daddy did not come along on the trip. They will have to pull it together, be responsible, and pay their own way, or turn around quickly and go home. I guess some would say it is time to grow up. We all would like to be like kids sometimes—have fun, and let someone else take care of the challenges, the bills, the car problems, etc. However, if we will determine to enjoy all the responsibilities that come with being an adult, as well as the freedoms, we can truly have a good time.

Confidence comes in knowing that we have prepared in advance, to the best of our ability, to take care of whatever needs may arise. So congratulate yourself in the great job you are now doing. No longer are you putting off to the last minute getting ready to go. Say "adios amigo" and go for it."

WHAT DID YOU SAY?

Have you ever said "yes" to something and later regretted saying it? Practice asking yourself, "What did I say?" We all have to watch our mouth. Just saying the simple word "yes" to a request will cost us something, one way or the other, "sooner or later", in the future.

Tonight I find myself away from home on a business trip that has cost me dearly. The biggest expense is my time. Is it profitable for my family? I don't think so. Is it costing them? Yes, precious moments of time that will never able to be created again. Heartbeats that will not be replaced; they are spent forever.

At times we may fail to realize that the choices we make can or will affect the lives of others...

Why am I here? I opened my big mouth that is why. Someone asked if I were willing to help work on the tables during a seminar. Without giving it the proper thought—counting the cost for fuel, time away from my family, and all the mileage on my car—I just said, "Sure." What was I thinking? Who knows? I definitely was not paying attention. I surely was not taking care of business in the sense of deciding if this were a wise decision. Instead of taking time to think when I was asked, I just quickly agreed. I did not want to have to take care of all the details right then, and be responsible—perhaps saying "No". Instead, here I am, dealing with the reality of not being home.

Now "later" has arrived! I am obligated to work the booth for nothing. And I find myself resenting the fact that I am in this situation because of procrastination in a different form. "I see the light! Stop making commitments without counting the cost! Watch what you say until you take the time to see exactly what you are getting yourself into. Do not put off checking all the details before you commit yourself."

It is better to count the cost, to wait and choose properly, than it is to find yourself in a place of frustration and disappointment later. At times, the cost might be very expensive, not only in the financial area, but in the emotional area as well. At times we may fail to realize that the choices we make can or will affect the lives of others—in this case, my family. I have learned from this lesson and I will strive in the future to watch what I say.

7
Taking Time to Reflect

COLD AS ICE

Have you ever felt numb on the inside? It's as if someone turns off a switch and all your emotions freeze up. Denial kicks in because you are not sure how to deal with the reality you sense has taken place. Someone asks you if you are OK and you say, "I'm fine." You have just lied to yourself and someone else, although you didn't even think twice before you spoke. You are on autopilot. Another person comes along and asks, "How are you?" Again, you respond with "I'm OK," although you feel as if you are dying inside. Oh, that smiley face mask you made fits you so well. Has it been permanently cemented on to cover the real you underneath? So, what does this have to do with procrastination?

Shakespeare said it right when he stated, "To thine own self be true." If we are not honest with ourselves, how can we be honest with others? You may be thinking, "I don't lie to people!" Hopefully, none of us would intentionally desire to be dishonest with others. At this moment, what I am addressing is being honest with ourselves.

If you find yourself troubled about something—something that keeps churning on the inside, and you know it has affected you to the point that you need to address it—then you must make the needed changes, or perhaps remove yourself entirely from the particularly troubling situation. Have you put it off?

Here is an example: Someone needs to talk to her spouse about the way he speaks to her, but because of fear—fear of being misunderstood or rejected, or a multitude of other reasons—she hesitates. Maybe later, when he is in a better mood, she will say something. What happens if he does not get in a better mood? If she decides that tomorrow she will talk to him, when tomorrow comes she finds that he is in a good mood. Not wanting him to get angry when she brings up something that he may perceive as negative, she puts off the subject again. Days, weeks, and years go by as she waits for the right time to speak, as he continues to degrade or wound her with his words. Because she did not speak up, he crosses over the boundaries on a regular basis, wounding her continually. Yet she never speaks out. (These circumstances may apply to both males and females.)

Can you see how this now becomes such a regular way of life that is accepted it as normal. Many go through all the same motions—serving, cooking, cleaning—but their heart is far away. How did they get into this position? What was once a warm heart, full of love, now seems cold and lifeless. Is this relationship dead? What happened?

...procrastinating in the areas of relationships can be harmful to one's health.

Procrastination! By not dealing with another person at the time it is needed can be painful for a moment or painful for a lifetime. The moment one becomes aware of a problem is the moment one requires wisdom. The question may be: is it wise to speak up and address the issue now, or is it prudent to wait for a better time? In any event, it is important to have discernment. Everyone needs to be able to know the difference between wisdom, on the one hand, and, on the other, what could become one of those perpetual "put-offs" due to procrastination. For truly, there is a difference. Where wisdom is helpful, the "put-off" can be detrimental or disastrous to a relationship.

Beware of the thought pattern that sounds something like this: "I will deal with that later." Many deal with heart issues later by escaping into drugs, alcohol, busyness, adultery, work, etc. Those who do not show it on the outside may stuff their feelings inside and suffer with headaches, stomach aches, back aches, and various other physical symptoms.

The bottom line: procrastinating in the areas of relationships can be harmful to one's health. Yes, it is wise to have a cooling off period if a couple gets into a heated conversation. No one wants that cooling off to grow "Cold as Ice" toward the one they once loved so deeply.

We are created to love one another, yet it is true in any relationship that hard times come in the world we live in. Procrastinating in the area of honesty can be the most detrimental act one can commit against one's mate. There is an interesting aspect about denial and not addressing something that needs to be dealt with. We may actually think we are just being nice. After all, we do not want to hurt their feelings! Later when they ask, "What is wrong?" and our reply is, "Nothing," there is a problem. They know that is not the truth. If one would be honest with themselves, they would admit that there is a problem. Instead, one may begin withdrawing and feeling cold inside. So how can someone deal with that?

Today, you can choose to make some changes. Stop ignoring those feelings. They are trying to get your attention. If there are situations with your boss, your children, your mate, or a friend, the same principle applies. When thoughts keep coming to your mind to put off dealing with the issue, decide today that you are going to take some constructive action to correct the problem.

When I decide to be honest with myself, I can be honest with others.

It is true that no one can change somebody else, and at times it seems that only Divine intervention can help. Yet our job, ultimately, is to "show up and tell the truth." The rest of the story may not be up to you to write. In other words, you can only be responsible to do your part. In any relationship, two people are involved. When I decided to be honest with myself, I can be honest with others.

It will be amazing to see how much relationships can change for the better when we all do our part. As we stop procrastinating in areas of honest communication with others, and ourselves, the ice can begin to melt and the warmth of a strong, healthy relationship can emerge.

FINISH WHAT YOU START

Have you ever started a project and been really excited about doing it? You tell all your friends, "I am making this... or, I am building that...." Your friends are happy for you, telling you that they think it is great that you are trying to accomplish that particular task. You feel energetic and enthusiastic about getting started. The first step is to make a plan. What materials do you need and how much will it cost? How much time will it take to complete or accomplish the job? Do you need assistance to finish, or can you do it alone? If you will need the help of others, are they willing to help? Can you count on them? In the area of time requirements, will their calendar correspond with yours so that you all can get together at the same time?

OK, now that you have gone over all your plans, it's time to go ahead and get started. The excitement increases, and with money in hand you head to the store to get all your supplies. You sense a little adrenaline rush as you walk through the isles and fill your cart with the needed items. Once you are back home and all the bags are unpacked you sit down and rest. Ah, now comes the reality; time to work! But you're so tired from shopping all day you decide you will wait a little while before you start.

Warning:
Notice that the adrenaline rush has diminished.

The excitement is not quite as strong as it was. Now it comes down to the nitty-gritty. A friend calls to see how you are doing. They ask if you've started on your project. You explain that you are tired, and you are going to start first thing tomorrow. When the morning comes you get an urgent call, a friend has a flat tire and no spare, and requests a helping hand. Whoops, there goes your time to work on your project. You realize that the other person needs help, so you put off what you were going to do until later.

The next thing you know the kids need your help, the dog gets sick, and then the boss requires your attention at the office! The list can go on and on. The following week you stumble over a small pile in the corner and notice that it is some of the supplies you purchased. Your memory is jogged by seeing them, and you say, "Oh, wow, I was going to make that…, but I got so busy that I forgot all about it. I think that tomorrow I will start working on it." We all know what will happen tomorrow, right?

Another idea comes along. I think I will paint a picture. I have always wanted to paint. I love to paint. I need to start doing more things that are fun and relaxing. I believe painting would be a good stress reliever. You call your friends and say," I think I am going to start a painting!" Again your friends are happy about your decision and encourage you to go for it. You begin to look in the library for books about art. You spend hours shopping for the right brushes, paint, and a canvas. You decide whether you will paint with water color, oil, or acrylic. It's all so exciting, with so many beautiful pictures to paint everywhere. Finally you make your decisions, purchasing all the tools you will need, and you arrive home.

Dinner needs to be made, so you set aside your priceless new possessions, momentarily. The excitement increases, and you can't wait to start. The family requests your time, dishes have to be washed, and then the kids need to be put to bed. Finally you have a sacred moment to yourself. You put all your materials out on the table—books, paints, brushes, canvas. And then realize that you don't know where to start. A sense of fear arises—after all, you don't want to mess up that new canvas. What if you don't do a good job?

The unrealistic expectation that you have to be able to paint a beautiful painting on the first attempt is daunting. It has to turn out great; otherwise it would mean you are not a good painter! Then when others see it, you could be embarrassed. The next thing you know, the priceless possessions that you thought would give you pleasure and would be a great stress reliever turn out to be a burden before you even put a stroke of paint on the canvas!

A pang of guilt strikes as you think about all the money you spent on the materials you are now stashing away in the garage. You feel embarrassed because you told your friends and family you were going to be a painter. You do not know how to be kind to yourself and allow yourself the time to learn. You want to be good "instantly". "Why can't I paint a Rembrandt now?" Our culture of fast food and hurry, hurry, takes away the freedom and ability to relax as we learn. Some of us do not know how to give ourselves the grace to play, and to make mistakes while we are learning. So instead we quit before we even start.

Procrastination can bring feelings of failure, because something else was started and not finished.

Because we put off what can bring relaxation and pleasure, with time and patience, the materials are put on the shelf. Procrastination can bring feelings of failure, because something else was started and not finished. Then self recriminations arise every time we see the supplies sitting in the corner. The key to freedom is to give yourself permission to start again.

Also it is important to look at the length of one's to-do lists. Written, or unwritten, one may need to shorten the list to feel good about themselves; otherwise they may end up with a lot of half finished projects.

Be gentle with yourself. Give yourself permission to have fun learning, and be patient while you grow in talent. Enjoy seeing the fruit of the labor of your hands. If you paint something you don't like, you can toss it, or keep it to see progress in your next painting. It is O.K. to make mistakes; we all do, many times. There is a lot of empty canvas in the world. Canvas can represent many things in life. As you take time to express yourself and explore the beauty that is all around you, feel the freedom to capture it with your unique talents.

THE OLD QUILT

Here it is 11:50 p.m. I have heard it said that one key to success is to just "do it now." The good thing about now is that it is not "a while ago." Nor is it "in a minute." It is neither past nor future. "Now is just now." So here I am now writing at the midnight hour.

Why would I wait to write until my eyes are heavy and I need to go to sleep? Because earlier I was busy finishing a quilting project—one more thing completed! Yeah! Congratulations.

Be sure to take time to congratulate yourself when you experience success, no matter how big or small.

It is very important to acknowledge your successes. In this case, there was no more procrastination on the quilt. After all, you cannot use a quilt when it is half done. It would not be too comfortable with all those pins and needles still in it.

Previously I had been struggling with an old sewing machine that was built back in the 1900s. I did not want to give in to the reality that the machine had seen better days. After all, this machine was made out of metal. My sewing machine repair man told me that as long as it would do what I desired it to do, keep it as long as I can. These days, all the sewing machines are made out of plastic. Finally, I gave in and purchased a new machine. I spent hundreds of dollars for beautiful new material to make a king-sized quilt. I drove hundreds of miles and spent hours getting perfectly matched pieces of fabric. I picked out the curtains to match, even getting lampshades of the same color. I had a beautiful plan.

I spent a lot of time and energy cutting up all the fabric, and I was ready to start. "Oh, wait. Tomorrow I can start sewing; I need to go do an errand first." Days went by. Soon all the material was put out of the way. Spring came along, with work, school, and planting a garden. Summer distractions brought camping, swimming, and other outside activities. In the fall serious delays to my project arrived in the form of injuries from a motorcycle accident.

SOME THINGS 'SHOULD" BE PUT OFF

In hindsight, that was one of those times I wished I had procrastinated or put-off going somewhere. I knew in my heart that I wasn't supposed to go on that ride. I had a nice bike—it looked like a little chopper, with lots of chrome—and it fit me like a glove. I wanted to take off on the Forth of July weekend, for a ride over to the coast in Northern California. Despite the warnings from others, as well as knowing in my heart that I should not have gone, I did anyway. That particular decision ended up in with my crashing my bike on a very dangerous road, and later being told that the doctor's diagnosis was that I had destroyed all the nerves in my left leg. His prognosis was that there was no cure. I was wheelchair-bound, and in intense pain! I had put off heeding the warning signs, and I had proceeded to pay a very high price.

Through prayer and a lot of hard work, a year later, I was able to walk again with a cane. Now I am able to dance and sing and freely express myself, without the help of anyone or anything other than God. That was a hard lesson to learn, and yet, that I did. To be honest, making a quilt is a lot less dangerous, yet not as much fun! Nevertheless, while I was recovering, I still had to keep going to the University so that I could receive my Bachelor's degree. My days just kept getting crazier with no time to stop, if I was in a wheelchair or not.

The inexpensive bedspread I bought to use temporarily was eventually worn out, and the new material was no longer new. Everything for the quilt was still lying where I had left it, waiting to be sewn together. I had forgotten how to sew the pattern, and now would have to spend more time relearning.

It is never too late to start over.

As I think about my desire to finish what I started, and finish this book, I know I am committed to do so. It is never too late to start over. I just have to be determined to pick up where I left off, and do what it takes. This book is a lot like the quilt—little pieces written in so many different locations, on a variety of types of paper, big and small—paper napkins, scratch papers, the back of an envelope—yet they all have to be gathered together and put into a format that everyone can enjoy.

One of the important things to remember is not to procrastinate in taking all your important thoughts and compiling them into a meaningful message that others can understand. Whether it is a journal, or a to-do list, a book, a poem, or a play, the important thing is to complete the process, so that others can see the results. As in the case of the quilt, as individual pieces of material they are too small to keep someone warm. But once the pieces have been sewn together to make up the proper size, they will be useful for others to enjoy.

In the same way, whatever it takes to capture a thought and then have it written for all to read—that is the key to success as a writer. Words alone are inadequate to be of any use until they are put together and form that beautiful piece of art called communication—threading thoughts together, as in a beautiful quilt.

HOW LONG, HOW LONG?

When I was at the gym today, a young man asked me, "How is your book going?" My face turned red. He laughed and said, "I didn't forget." I tried to explain that I was on my last chapter, but that I had had to put it on hold. The reality of procrastinating on the last chapter of a book that deals with exactly that subject is humorous to say the least. Yet, as you can see by having this book in your hand, I finally succeeded in finishing that which I had started. How? I stopped putting it off any longer and, like a quilt, began piecing it all together.

At times I have to remind myself that everything takes time. If I take the time to add letters together they can make up a word. Adding words together, I can make up a sentence. As I add sentences together, they can make up a paragraph, that can become a chapter, and with time, a book. Knowing these simple truths, it still takes time to write, or create things we desire. I realize that I realistically will not have time to go away and write for months on end. Yet if I apply the theory below, it will eventually help me arrive to my desired destination.

Have you heard of the fifteen-minute theory? Needing to accomplish a certain goal, apply yourself to this end for only fifteen-minutes per day. Once you start, the majority of the time you will continue past the time allotted. If you have worked the whole fifteen minutes and want to stop, celebrate the fact that you made progress. (I like to use a timer, and then I race to see how much I can accomplish before the bell rings). Using the fifteen-minute theory five days a week will whittle down any project, as time passes and one continues to be faithful. This is one way to achieve another victory over the pitfalls resulting from put offs.

AGING & PROCRASTINATION

Writing this book has been of great benefit in helping me to push past what I thought was the end of my endurance. I kept thinking, "I am done. That's good enough." It caused me to see things in a different light in many areas. One area was realizing the fact that I am not going to live forever, so if I really was going to get this thing published, I had better focus on it and get it finished.

What started that line of reasoning was when I was asked the question, "How long would you like to live?" I have long life in my genes, grandma lived to be ninety-five and mom is eighty-three, so if I take care of my brain and body, I believe I can enjoy the length and quality of life I desire. At one time I calculated that if I lived to be eighty, how old my children and grandchildren would be, it was a mathematical adventure.

I have been blessed with five daughters, four grandsons, a great grandson, and one on the way! I desire to have some influence in their lives and to share some of the wisdom I have gained from living a long life.

One of the ways we can gain wisdom and knowledge is through reading. I have a collection of books, written in the nineteenth and early twentieth centuries, that I love. They reveal a part of life and history that is known only because the authors were faithful to take the time to write. I view it as a privilege and a responsibility to share with others what life was like living in the 1900s, now that we are living in the twenty-first century. I find it humorous when I am talking to someone and I make a comment similar to, "...that was back in the 1900s." They laugh and give me a funny look, as if that were a long time ago! Being born in the '50s, I have the advantage of living half-way through one era, and possibly half-way through the next.

...the opportunity of getting old is a privilege, not drudgery.

Many fear the idea of aging, and I do not honestly like the idea of getting all wrinkled and too tired to do anything, yet these thoughts come to mind. I view life as a gift from God. So the opportunity of getting old is a privilege, not drudgery. Truly, not everyone gets to be my age, so I should not complain. In the past I feared that I could get totally lazy and not take care of myself. It is so easy to think, "Tomorrow I will get back on track—I will eat right, etc., but for now I just want…. All my life I have been health conscious and I have exercised; yet the day came when I started slipping up. What happened? Age, lack of time, procrastination all played a part. I know that for sure!

As a student in night school, and one suffering from insomnia due to menopause, sound sleep was not something I was able to experience. My body was going through changes, hot flashes in class, challenges in a variety of ways, plus my memory seemed to be fading. This all seemed like great reasons to put-off going to the gym.

As a younger woman I had always been into doing things naturally; I even home-birthed my last three babies. I thought that was challenging, but it was nothing compared to this new adventure. I keep thinking I will wake up and the ride will be over, yet here comes another heat wave. Is it hot in here or is it just me?

The weight gain is also scary: "What happened to my figure?" The doctors told me that it is normal for many women to gain an average of twenty pounds when they go through menopause. That is not encouraging news to me; unfortunately I could not put this process off.

Taking care of our health should always be a top priority. I had to realize that no matter how important other things are that I committed to take care of, if I do not take care of myself I will not be able to help others. For some reason, a lot of people feel guilty if they take time to take care of themselves. There is a time, and best for everyone, when you put on hold other things and just take care of yourself. And there is a balance that is important to find, especially in this area. Health consciousness promotes our physical well-being and enhances prospects for longevity. This is the best health insurance we can give ourselves—especially as we grow older.

I personally do not believe this life is a dress rehearsal. Therefore, as I am aging, I do not want to procrastinate in the area of exploration. I desire to travel and to take time to enjoy some time by myself, as well as with others, in new and adventurous places.

Life choices you and I make now will help prepare us for future years.

As I get older, I desire to see myself practice being more balanced while using my time to work and play. I realize that my mind can plan all kinds of things. Yet as I age, my body is letting me know that it has greater limitations than it used to. Although I see myself as energetic, adventurous, and desiring to continue traveling and teaching, I may need to change some of those plans, and realistically practice self-care, balanced with work, writing, art, music, or other things I love.

Life choices you and I make now will help prepare us for future years. First, I personally believe it is important to take time for prayer and meditation daily. Secondly, it is important to take good care of our health and fitness needs according to doctor's reports:

- Get a minimum of 8 hours of sleep each night.
- Proper nutrition and flossing your teeth improves overall health.
- Exercise.
- Balance time spent in work, play, and rest.
- Live within realistic time frames and expectations.

I believe that by making the needed adjustments to keep our health and fitness we can reap many benefits as we continue to age.

As we grow older, we are continually changing. Everything changes all the time—the weather, the seasons, people, our jobs, our moods, the places we live, etc. I am reminded not to try to hold onto anything for stability, for it too, whatever it is, will change. I believe that God is the only one who never changes, and that is the only security I can depend on. The future has many adventures to enjoy, as well as many twists, turns, and turmoil. As we learn to embrace life—and not put off things- this will help us grow old with grace.

Remember to be gentle with yourself. Learn to focus. Accept your human limitations. Be content. Finish what you start. As you enjoy the journey, and stay on the right path for your personal life, you can follow through and finish the race. Wonderful joy is experienced with the knowledge and satisfaction that what was started has been completed.

I encourage you to share with others your victories and celebrations over areas in your life that were once tormented by procrastination. This is a new beginning for the rest of your life.

As we learn to embrace life— and not put off things—this will help us grow old with grace.

The Grand Finale

The ultimate challenge of a procrastinator is to finish what they start.

"THE GRAND FINALE"

As I was in the process of writing this book, life continually seemed to be consumed with everything but the opportunity to write on this topic. Getting an education is one example. Did I procrastinate way back in the day? No, the thought of going to school was not even in my mind. I was busy raising five daughters and homeschooling them.

In the midst of taking care of things at home and working, I went back to school. At the same time, I entered into new transitions with the empty nest syndrome. Yet small pieces of this book continued to be scribbled down on pieces of paper here and there. I would write down quick thoughts while waiting in lines, waiting at stoplights when traveling, while standing in the bank, in restaurants, and numerous other locations. In addition, there were a variety of coffee shops I went to as I worked on these pages and purposely moved forward to see this book progress in its creation.

The question arises, how could one stop writing about a continually emerging topic? The subject of procrastination can go on indefinitely, for we all are subject to the challenges that come with it. When I told other people I was writing a book titled "Pitfalls from Put-Offs", but I was stuck on the last chapter, they always laughed. The ultimate challenge of a procrastinator is to finish what they start.

As human beings, it is part of our nature, at times, to put off anything that is not pleasant nor instantly rewarding. Nevertheless, we can walk in freedom and enjoy life...

Many examples have been given in these stories. Although this is not a "How to Stop Procrastinating" book, clues and tips were given along the way. One last thing I will say is this: You can be successful and can make great changes in your life. Now you can see yourself from a new point of view. In the light of truth and inspiration, you can experience new adventures with new outlooks. As human beings, it is part of our nature, at times, to put off anything that is not pleasant or instantly rewarding. Nevertheless, we can walk in freedom and enjoy life, as we continue to see things in new perspectives. I want to congratulate you for following through to the very end of this book. That in itself reveals the fact you completed a new task. You finished what you started!

It is time for you to begin a new journey with the possibility of great changes in your future. With yesterday past, and tomorrow not yet here, *now* is the time to celebrate life, with all of its triumphs and challenges. We all at one time or another choose, either purposefully or unintentionally, to procrastinate. That is why it is helpful to talk with others—to get feedback, encouragement, or even to have someone we can be accountable to. At times we all need someone who will help us address an area that we would rather not deal with until later. So it is in life.

Remember, we are all in this together. I believe you are taking the next step towards your success. Congratulations, as you move forward in your new-found freedom from the pitfalls from put-offs!

I am proud of you. I know you can do it.

Brenda

www.ingramcontent.com/pod-product-compliance
Ingram Content Group UK Ltd.
Pitfield, Milton Keynes, MK11 3LW, UK
UKHW041954230426
12048UKWH00008B/342